Christian Ways to Date, Go Steady, and Break Up

by John Butler

illustrated by Duane Orlemann

STANDARD PUBLISHING
Cincinnati, Ohio

39949

The following abbreviations are used to identify the Scripture versions quoted:

NIV—*New International Version,* © 1973 by New York Bible Society International, used by permission.

NASB—*New American Standard Bible,* © The Lockman Foundation 1960, 1962, 1963, 1968, 1971, 1973, 1975, used by permission.

2nd Edition, 1985

Library of Congress Cataloging in Publication Data

Butler, John, 1949-
   Christian ways to date, go steady, and break up.

   Summary: Discusses the process of dating including asking for a date and dissolving a relationship while maintaining your Christian attitudes and behavior.
   1. Dating (Social Customs). 2. Dating (Social Customs)—Religious aspects—Christianity.
[1. Dating (Social Customs)   2. Christian life]
I. Title.
HQ801.B895   1985   646.7'7   85-8139
ISBN 0-87239-986-9

Does anyone have a perfect dating life? Whether your problem is getting a date, keeping a date, going steady, pain or fear of breaking up, or maintaining Christian attitudes and behavior throughout the whole process, this book is for you.

Introduction

This book covers a broad spectrum of the dating life. It will be beneficial for non-daters, occasional daters, regular daters, and steady couples. The point is, no one should stop reading because he has "never had a date," or "is already going steady." Everyone will learn something.

About the Questions to Consider

While this book is grounded in Scripture, it contains very little moralizing and preaching. This is done for two reasons:

1. The morality and ethics of the content is fairly obvious;

2. Different churches and socio-economic areas have different dating customs and rules. It is better to leave such conclusions up to you. For instance, among a group of aspiring professionals (those who plan to be doctors, professors, etc.), marriage before age 24 might be impractical. On the other hand, in some communities, marriage at age 18—20 might not only be normal, but practical. Therefore, these questions are designed to let you arrive at the conclusions best suited to you.

The questions, mini-dramas, and projects can be approached in any of several ways if you want to use this book as a group study, including:

1. Ask your choice of questions to the group at large and let them discuss the questions together.

2. Divide into small groups to discuss different questions. Then have each of the small groups report its opinion to the group at large.

3. Assign each person a question to think over (for a few minutes or for the next week) and then report his opinion to the class.

Mini-Dramas

These provide opportunity to simulate conditions mentioned in a particular chapter. Again, there are different approaches possible for their execution:

1. Pick out established couples to *ad lib* a particular situation in front of the group.

2. Let "dramatists" break into small groups to organize their story lines. Then come back together for the performances.

3. Assign couples to write up small drama scripts during the week and perform them as readers' theater at the next class session.

Projects

These are designed to gain additional insight from outside research, and "to put theory to the test"—to actually attempt and experience situations mentioned in the chapters. Basically, the projects turn "nice thoughts" into real-life situations.

Chapter One: BREAKING THE ICE

JIM AND CHERI SAT ON THE PARK BENCH UNDER THE MOON- LIGHT. They talked in romantic, hushed tones about ... who knows what? Jim bent close to Cheri and gave her a friendly nibble on the ear lobe. Cheri responded with a resounding backhand across Jim's face. *I've gotta work on my timing*, he thought ....

Fred has a "mad crush" on Myrtle. He makes dinner reservations for two at the fancy French restaurant downtown for seven o'clock, Saturday night. He approaches Myrtle in the hall at school between classes.

"Uh, hi. Ummm. Whatter-ya doin' Saturday night?" he stammers.

"What's it to you?" she snaps back, and proceeds to her class.

"Let's see, I wonder what I did wrong?" Fred mumbles to himself as he stands alone, shaking his head....

Alice is good-looking, witty, has a nice figure, is intelligent, talented, musical, and has an upstanding moral character. But she never gets asked out, even by the guys at her church. This is really strange. After all, she really is good-looking, witty, intelligent, talented, and musical. Alice even explains these facts to her friends all the time. Why she is never asked out remains a mystery....

Dating is like driving a car. It's a common activity, but it takes only a small mistake to upset the process. With cars, it can be grease on the points, bad timing, too little water in the radiator, or too much dirt in the air cleaner. With dating, it can also be "bad timing," an ego problem (in either direction), or a wrong approach. To use another metaphor, it doesn't take a very big "foul" to send you to the penalty box in the dating game.

As Alice has shown us, your dating life doesn't begin the first time you ask somebody out or vice versa. Success in asking someone out or in getting asked out depends largely on your dress, grooming, behavior, and speech habits. These factors in turn are largely determined by your concept of yourself. And your self-concept will probably reflect your relationship to the Lord and to His Word.

For instance, if Jim had a little more respect for Cheri's feelings and less preoccupation with his own "moves," not only would he have remained unslapped, he would have better represented Christ. If Fred realized that Jesus commands us to love ourselves in order to love our neighbors, he wouldn't be so squeamish and evasive when talking to Myrtle. He might have had a date by now. If Alice were secure in the gifts and talents the Lord has given her, she would not have the compulsion to vocally advertize her assets.

All the dating tactics in the world won't give you a good dating life unless they are based on a personality marked by *honest selflessness* and *objective self-examination.* Who likes to be around those who express only preoccupation with their own concerns? Sensitivity to others' needs *(selflessness)* prevents that from happening. An attitude of selflessness

10

helps turn you into the kind of person people like to be with and go out with. Who is attracted to the unkempt, the complainer, the egotist? *Objective self-examination* is important. Look at yourself. Listen to yourself, especially when you are out among people. The information you gather will explain the present status of your dating life, whether good or bad.

If, after reading this book, your dating life is still not enhanced, come back to this chapter and honestly evaluate yourself: *Am I lovable?* That's where it all starts.

In the meantime, let's get on with it. The place to start in dating survival tactics is with conversational habits. There are two main problems one encounters in talking to members of the opposite sex:

1. When males talk to each other, subject matter often deals with cars, sports, work, and girls. Their manner tends to be coarse, if not downright crude. When females talk to each other, subject matter tends toward clothes, make-up, sewing, other people, and boys.

Their manner is often cliquish. Obviously, if the two sexes retain these speech habits when they talk to each other, there will be a clash.

2. Because of problem #1, guys and girls are often self-conscious when they talk to each other, and self-consciousness often brings foolish behavior with it.

Notice how even these problems peculiar to guy-girl conversation stem from self-centeredness. The apostle Paul tells Christians to "Do nothing from selfishness or empty conceit ... do not merely look out for your own personal interests, but also for the interests of others" (Philippians 2:3, 4, NASB). Once again, attitude is more important than "tips" on behavior, because attitudes will determine technique.

Guys: For instance, if you're concerned about the girl's feelings, you won't find yourself talking and joking to her in a crude manner. Neither will you poke or tickle her when the conversation dwindles. Being crude around a girl is "selfishness or empty conceit." Rather, you should want to ask the girl questions designed to find out what *she* is like. Rambling on about your experiences in auto maintenance or weight-lifting is not "looking out for the interests of others."

Girls: If you are primarily concerned about the feelings of the guy you are talking to, you will not act "catty" or "tsk" or roll your eyes or do any number of nonverbal gestures that can make a guy feel ill at ease. You, too, will look to his interests, which means putting away preoccupations with your nails, hair, or homework.

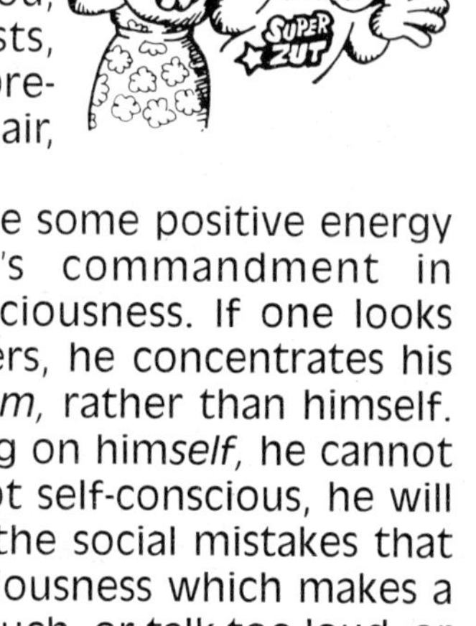

Instead, we should generate some positive energy toward each other. Paul's commandment in Philippians defeats self-consciousness. If one looks out for the interests of others, he concentrates his attention and energy on *them*, rather than himself. And if he is not concentrating on him*self*, he cannot be *self*-conscious. If one is not self-conscious, he will probably not exhibit any of the social mistakes that accompany it. It is self-consciousness which makes a person clam up, or talk too much, or talk too loud, or talk only about himself (wants to stick with familiar subject matter). This same little social disease also produces giggling, red faces, and extremely strange subjects of conversation (sometimes fear of "dead air" results in noise for noise's sake).

So, if you get nervous talking to the opposite sex, take some time first to think about *that* person, and to forget yourself. Find out some of the things they are interested in and things they do. You'll be amazed at the difference it makes in the way you get along and are accepted by others.

One of the most nervous times in a boy/girl encounter is when one asks the other for a date for the first time. While "looking out for the other person's interests" is important, it is also important to know what you're doing. The following sequence of events should help. While the things to remember may be fairly obvious, the sequence shown here is important. (For instance, you shouldn't arrange for transportation or buy the tickets a week after you've asked her.)

Drumming Up a First Date

Step 1: WHO? Decide first on the girl you want to take out. (Occasionally, a really fantastic event may come along, in which case you decide "what" before "who.") She will probably be someone you find attractive—someone you know, but not well enough. Hopefully, your attraction to this person will be based partially on her moral character and relationship to Christ. If she possesses neither of these attributes, re-check your motives.

Step 2. WHAT? Decide **what** you would like to do on the date. Select an activity that is readily acceptable, such as a movie or a basketball game. A common, inexpensive activity minimizes self-consciousness and the tendency to "perform" for each other. Since this is a first date, choose an activity that gives you opportunity to talk to each other and to emphasize things you have in common.

Step 3: WHERE? Decide **where** the date will take place. If you choose dinner-

and-a-movie, the choice is largely yours. If you pick a football game, the location has been determined for you by the league commissioner.

Step 4: WHEN? Establish the **day and time** when you want to go out. Also, at this step, figure alternatives in case you get turned down at any point: (alternate girl, activity, place, and time). If this is a special event such as a concert or reserved-seat affair, buy the tickets now, or make reservations. This is also the time to arrange for transportation if you don't have a car.

Step 5. WILL YOU? *Ask her.* This step may well be the "trickiest" part of the whole process for two reasons: 1) no opportunity to ask her properly; 2) fear of rejection.

To solve problem #1, plan to ask her at a time when no one is listening in, and when there is enough time to get the job done comfortably. If no situation fits those requirements during the day, use the telephone in the evening.

To solve problem #2, avoid "feeler" questions such as "Do you like miniature golf?" and the classic, "What are you doing Saturday night?" Notice how these "feeler" questions are aimed at one *aspect* of the date, rather than at the date itself. Her personal habits and schedule are none of your business. SPEAK UP AND ASK HER FOR THE DATE. Relax. Be casual. She's just another human being who happens to be female. If you talk too loud and fast, she will back off as if you were a door-to-door salesman. If you mumble and leave out details, she may decide it's not worth the trouble to find out what you want.

Ask her a few days in advance of the event itself. If homecoming is on Friday, don't wait until Thursday to ask somebody. On the other hand, if you want to take a girl window shopping, don't ask her two weeks in advance. The more elaborate and socially oriented the date is, the earlier you should ask. For casual dates, allow one to five days.

She may want to go out with you, but may object to

the date because of a conflict in time or something. That is why you have a back-up plan. If you can tell that she really wants to go, especially if *she* suggests an alternative, try to work it out. But don't be a doormat for her schedule. Girls get tired of doormats very quickly.

Step 6: "YES!"

ZACKY: Zelda, will you go to the homecoming with me?

ZELDA: O.K.

ZACKY: Wow! You mean it? I mean, you aren't kidding? Really? Zowie!

ZELDA: Hmmm. I think I just changed my mind.

If she accepts your invitation, don't "blow your cover" with a response like Zacky's. She might wonder what is so strange about you that makes dates such a jubilant surprise.

DORIS: Where's this movie playing, anyway?

LENNY: At the *Ritz.*

DORIS: You mean it's not at the *Cheapo?*

LENNY: No. It's at the *Ritz.*

DORIS: I was all ready to go in my overalls, but I guess I'll wear a dress instead.

Be sure to give the necessary details to keep the date smooth. Tell her if special clothing is required. Doris and Lenny show us that dinner-and-a-movie can range from overalls to long dresses, depending on the style of restaurant and the prestige of the theater.

Step 6a: "no." What to do if she turns you down.

Don't fall apart yet. There are two kinds of "no's": 1)

"Don't ask me again," and 2) "Circumstances beyond my control prevent me from going with you to this particular event." Learn how to distinguish the difference. Here are some examples:

"No" for now.
—"I have plans that night, but it sounds like it would be fun."
—"No; I have a class that night. How about Thursday instead?" (If she suggests the alternative, you *know* she wants to go out with you.)
—"I don't like Chinese food, but ask me again when you feel like steak."

"No" for good.
—A sweet smile accompanied by a shake of the head, "no."
—"Maybe some other time," or "Could we make it another time?" These are both examples of indefinite procrastination. Putting something off indefinitely equals "never."
—"I have plans that night." Period. End of discussion.
—"I hate Chinese food." Period. No explanation.
—"I'm going steady," or "Ask my boyfriend." Stay away.
Note: If you are turned down, do not ask her, "Why?" She doesn't owe you an explanation just because you asked her for a date.

Step 7: PLAN "B." If you still feel like going out, ask someone else. Suit the activity to the individual's personality. And don't tell girl "B" that she is girl "B." That sort of "honesty" is self-destructive, hurts her feelings, and leaves you without a date. Again.

Getting Asked Out

Step 1: LISTEN! Listen attentively while he's asking you. Don't shut him off. Hear him out, even if you have already decided he's a "flake." You might want to change your mind.

Step 2: WHO is this guy? While he is asking, decide whether you want to go out with him at all. Is your reasoning fair to both of you? Will your relationship to Christ suffer if you go out with him?

Step 3: WHAT are we doing? Do you want to participate in the date he's suggesting? Have you been waiting for a chance to go to the symphony? Or is it a gory movie you would rather not see? Does Mexican food make you sick? If a personal conflict with the activity is the only issue, let him know that you are turning down the *activity* and not *him* as a person.

Step 4: WHEN is this date? Do you have a conflict with the time he has suggested? If you would like to go out with him but time is the only conflict, let him know. Maybe the two of you can work out an alternate suitable time together.

Step 5: "YES!" Obviously, if you have no conflicts about his character or the date itself, accept. Don't act too nonchalant about accepting the date. Too nonchalant says that you don't really care if you go. Most fellows are scared of being "taken for a ride." On the other hand, acting *too* glad or surprised either says that "you've got the 'hots' for him," or that dates are rare for you and therefore you must be "weird."

Step 5a: "no." **How to say it.** There's no big trick to turning down a date in such a way that the guy will know that you still want to go out with him. Just let him know that you have a conflict with the activity or the time slot he suggested. You might even suggest an alternate activity or time, which should remove any doubt about whether you want to go out with him.

The big problem is when someone you don't like or want asks you out. As a Christian, you don't want to hurt him. But you don't want to lie to him either. Jesus said to "let your 'Yes' be 'Yes' and your 'No,' 'No'" (Matthew 5:37,NIV). In other words, give a simple, straight answer, and let your actions back up what you say. That means that if you want to turn him down for good, be friendly, but don't flirt. Girls often tell "white lies" to turn down a date nicely. This creates more problems than it solves. It is best not to say:

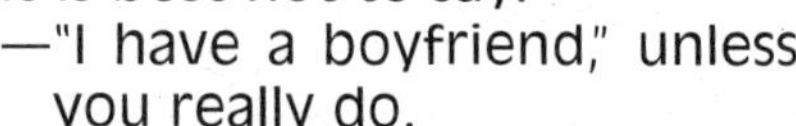

—"I have a boyfriend," unless you really do.
—"I have plans that evening," because he'll probably believe you and ask you out again later.
—"Maybe some other time." This only puts the problem off. He'll probably take you literally.

—"Are you kidding?" Or "What? With *you?*" or anything else that is sarcastic or insulting. For one thing, it's un-Christlike. Besides that, just because he may not be good for you doesn't mean that he's no good at all.

—"Why don't you ask out Julie?" That's the ultimate insult; it is saying, "You're out of my league, kid."

—"I don't like Chinese food." You're evading the issue. Never assume that "he can take a hint." When a guy is really attracted to a girl, "hope springs eternal." That is why your turndown must not be ambiguous.

Instead, "Let your conversation be always full of grace, seasoned with salt, so that you may know how to answer everyone" (Colossians 4:6, NIV). A simple "No, I don't think so," or "No, thank you" should convey the message without being cruel. You may even have to say, "You and I are good friends now. Let's not ruin it by getting romantic." He may act hurt for a while, but there's no use feeling guilty about your

being honest in a matter you can't help. Rejection never does feel good, but it feels worse to get insincere answers and uncertainty. And if he really "causes a scene" when you turn him down, shrug it off. He's just confirmed your decision.

As a Christian, you have a responsibility to base your decision on what you really know about the guy, and not on the slander and gossip that often goes around.

Now, in order to shake off the last few paragraphs of negative subject matter (getting turned down), and to get back to the purpose of this study, which is to *date*, not to turn somebody down, let's say that (if you're a guy) you've asked the girl out and she's agreed to go. And, (if you're a girl) a guy in whom you are interested (mildly to wildly) has just ask you out; you have no unresolvable conflicts, and you've agreed to go. What then? Well, that comes in the next chapter.

#1

Questions to Consider

Questions 1—3 are designed to compare (and contrast) typical boy/girl "game-playing" with Christian ethics. Questions 4—9 should lead into insights which could not be obtained in a book. Questions 4—9 should also become an open forum for boys and girls to air their expectations in dating to each other. All of the questions should be helpful to stimulate your thinking.

1. Is it dishonest to present your "good side" first, i.e., not to act nervous when you really are, etc.?

2. What are the advantages in adjusting your conversation and interests to the person you are talking to? What are some possible disadvantages?

3. Is it ever right to lie when turning down a date? If so, when and why? If not, why not?

4. Girls: Would you accept a date with a handicapped person? Crippled? Blind? Palsied? Deaf? Amputee? Dwarfed? Would your decision really "depend on what kind of person he is," or is that just an excuse? Why or why not accept such a date?

5. Guys: Would you ask out a handicapped girl? Why or why not? Do you have an obligation as a Christian to ask one out? Does it bother you that such girls may never have a date in their lives? What can be done about it?

6. Girls: Give some reasons why you would refuse a date.

7. Guys: Give some characteristics a girl might have that would keep you from asking her out.

8. Girls: Give some reasons you would accept a first date, especially from someone you don't know too well.

9. Guys: Give some reasons you would want to ask a girl out.

Mini-Dramas

1. Choose a boy and a girl from the group. Have them pretend they are strangers who have just met:
   a. at a basketball game.
   b. at work.
   c. in class.
   d. at a church youth party.
2. Choose another girl and guy from the group. Have the guy simulate asking the girl to a high-school basketball game in the following situations:
   a. on the telephone.
   b. between classes at school.
   c. seeing her by chance at a shopping mall.
   In each case, have the girl opt to:
   a. accept.
   b. turn him down because of a conflict in time.
   c. turn him down because she doesn't like him.

Chapter Two:
WHAT TO DO ON A FIRST DATE

NORMAN: Aaaah! My first date with Sherry. It'll be a classic: Dinner and movie. I've been wanting to take this doll baby out for weeks.

At the restaurant:

SHERRY: (to herself) Boy! He sure gobbles his food. MUNCH MUNCH MUNCH.

NORMAN: (to himself) Boy! At these prices she'd better finish what she ordered! (out loud) Pass the ketchup.

SHERRY: Here.

At the theater:

NORMAN: Funny, huh?

SHERRY: Yeah.

Driving home:

NORMAN: Sure was some movie, huh?

SHERRY: Yeah.

NORMAN: G'night.

SHERRY: G'night.

On the way back to his house.

NORMAN: Aaaah! My last date with Sherry.

Have you ever had a first date similar to Norman and Sherry's experience? Have you never had a first date because you're afraid this is what would happen? First dates *can* be good. There are some very simple principles in dating and conversation which can help you avoid washout dates.

Spectate or Participate? There are two basic kinds of dates:

1. The one in which you sit and watch (spectate).
2. The ones in which you creatively provide recreation for yourselves (participate).

The first group includes movies, plays, concerts, watching TV, listening to records, and watching sports events. The second group includes playing miniature golf, tennis, Ping-Pong, volleyball, canoeing, skiing (either kind), boating, art galleries, zoos, and museums. In group 1, the two of you sit and watch. In group 2, you do something relaxing, invigorating, and/or creative together. There are assets and liabilities for both categories. Let's look at 'em.

"Spectator" Dates. *Advantages.* The big advantages for spectator dates are that they are 1) common, 2) popular, and 3) fun. If you have two tickets for Bruce Springsteen or the current Oscar-winning movie, chances are you will have little trouble finding someone to go along. The same might not be true if you said, "Let's go canoeing!" So the big advantage to spectator amusements is that everybody likes to go to them. They are good for a "first date" because there is no cause for embarrassment. Since spectating consists of sitting and watching, it is something nearly everyone knows how to do. But before you go out and buy your tickets, remember that spectator amusements also have their

Disadvantages. 1) They are expensive. (Have you priced a live pop or rock concert lately?) 2) All you do is sit and watch, which in turn can produce the following results: a) sitting and watching most events allows little chance for conversation. Thus, it defeats one of the main purposes of a first date—to get to know someone better. b) We sit and watch too much already; sitting and watching does nothing to raise self-esteem, it seldom aids in growth in creativity, and a couple can get tired of each other sooner that way than if they are doing something together.

"Participation" Dates. *Advantages.* Participation dates 1) relieve boredom and allow an outlet for otherwise wasted creative energy. 2) They help delay sexual temptations because the couple are focusing their energy on an external outlet. 3) Participation affirms self-esteem and develops skills and insights. 4) It is less self-centered in nature. 5) On the average, participation dates cost less than spectator amusements. 6) Most activities allow plenty of time for conversation and tension release; hence, it is easier to get to know each other. The

Disadvantages of participation really reside in the hang-ups and laziness of the would-be participants, not in the activities themselves. The first disadvantage is that people lack the inclination to get out and do anything. How many people would rather go canoeing or hiking than watch TV or a movie? The second disadvantage is self-consciousness in competitive games. A novice bowler, for instance, may not have much of a thrill competing with someone with an average of 243.

While we could probably figure out some more advantages for spectator amusements, they would probably be weaker than the six in favor of active, participation dates. Therefore, for a first date, if you can get by with a participation date without getting strange looks from your would-be partner, go for it. In fact, try to let participation outnumber spectator dates by about three to one.

There is one other kind of date that is in a class by itself· the Big Social Event. This includes homecoming, banquets—anything that involves people getting together, is expensive, and dressy. Often, these constitute first dates for many of the participants.

For a big social event to be a first date, the advantages include 1) security in having an escort; 2) time and opportunity to talk to your partner; 3) you're among friends who may make you feel more comfortable. The disadvantages include 1) it's often expensive—you may not want to sink that much money into your first date with someone (Total bills for Jr./Sr. Prom often reach $250.00 each); 2) there is pressure to impress each other when you are so dressed up (This often leads to self-consciousness and blunders.); 3) being among people you know may make you feel *un*comfortable—"Well, look who's going around together!"

How to Talk on a First Date. At the beginning of the chapter, Norman and Sherry made two mistakes in their first (and probably last) date together. The first, which we discussed, was in not selecting an activity conducive to conversation. Their second mistake was in ignoring a simple rule when beginning conversation: Ask questions that evoke explanations! For instance, suppose Norman had asked Sherry, "What did you like about the movie?" rather than, "Some movie, huh?" The conversation on the way home might have been more interesting and communicative. Rather than ask "Yes" or "No" questions, ask "Why," "How," "Which," or "What do you think?":

—"Why didn't you like Hoboken?"
—"How does macrame work?"
—"Which parts of the movie upset you?"
—"What do you think the Christian's responsibility is toward inner-city poverty?"

Such questions have positive results: 1) They get the other person talking or communicating (which is better than you rambling on about yourself); 2) it lets you truly learn something about the other person; 3) it raises your date's self-esteem because you are demonstrating a genuine interest in his/her mind; 4) it helps eliminate "dead air." Silence between two people who know each other can be peaceful, but silence between two people together for the first time creates anxiety, nervousness, and consequent social blunders.

Subject Matter. Anything that is of interest to both of you, and upon which you concur, should do as conversational subject matter for your first date. Controversial subjects are probably best left to close friends. Be positive in your conversation. Gossiping and talking about negative things, especially in a judgmental tone, is depressing and destructive. Ephesians 4:29, 31 says, "Do not let any unwholesome talk come out of your mouths, but only what is helpful for building others up according to their needs, that it may benefit those who listen. Get rid of all bitterness, rage and anger, brawling and slander, along with every form of malice" (NIV). No matter how true or justified a person's negative feelings may be toward something or someone, habitually venting negative attitudes drags down yourself and your companion(s). Besides, the persons talked about usually find out anyway. Gossip is altogether an effective way to eventually gain solitude.

How to Act on a First Date. As was mentioned in chapter one, remembering "do's" and "don't's" on dating behavior won't help as much as developing the right attitude. The right attitude is found in Philippians 2:3, "Do nothing from selfishness or empty conceit, but with humility of mind let each of you regard one another as more important than himself" (NASB). Forget yourself. Don't worry about whether you think you're dumb, or too fat, or too flat, or that you've got a lot of homework to do yet. Become unconscious of self, and the symptoms of self-consciousness disappear.

To Kiss or Not to Kiss. Randy and Lisa were on their first date together. As Randy walked Lisa home, he thought, *Lisa is a nice girl; we've had a friendly time; I'd like to hold her hand. Maybe sneak a kiss at the door.* He reached and took Lisa's hand.

Ooooh! Lisa thought in response, *He must really like*

me a lot. When Randy *kissed* her at the door, she wondered when he would be giving her his ring.... Randy left Lisa's house thinking, *That was a nice, friendly date. I'm sure glad I'm not tied down to anybody.*

The point in the above episode is not that kissing and holding hands on a first date is a "no-no." But it can be tricky. The significances of these two acts of affection vary from person to person. Suppose, for example, that Lisa had kissed only one other boy in her life, and that was when she was going steady with him. Then her assumptions with Randy are easy to understand. And maybe Randy has been accustomed to good-night kisses on first dates. To him, a first-date peck means nothing more than affectionate friendship. This does not mean that he "leads girls on." But if these two attitudes meet, the girl might think she's found her new love, while the boy has no such intention. He will then pull away from her and think, *She tries to latch onto every guy who's nice to her.* Lisa, on the other hand, will think, *So, he didn't like me at all! He was just out for sex.*

Obviously, neither perception is entirely accurate. Generally speaking, guys tend to seek affection because it is "fun." Girls more often associate affection with "love." Either way, do not assume that your date attaches the same significance to holding hands or kissing that you do.

One More Thing. When a newly dating couple becomes too affectionate too soon, conversation dwindles; sometimes it nearly stops. This defeats the primary purpose of dating—getting to know someone better. This is not to prohibit holding hands or kissing on the first date, but abstinence or healthy temperance certainly develops better balanced relationships. A perfectly good dating arrangement can be ruined if it is preoccupied by "making out."

#2

Questions to Consider

1. Is it all right to date someone you would never marry? Why or why not?

2. Would you accept (or ask for) a casual date with a non-Christian?

3. What's the biggest problem for you on a first date? Have you found any ways to solve it?

4. What do you want a first date to accomplish?

5. What does kissing mean to you personally? Does it depend on the circumstances? Is that all right?

6. What is your favorite kind of date with someone you don't know well yet?

7. How old should a guy be to start dating? Should he be able to drive?

8. How old should a girl be to start dating?

9. Do you think earlier dating leads to earlier marriages?

10. Describe the worst first impression you ever made on a first date. How much was your fault? How much was due to circumstances?

11. What was the best first date you ever had? What made it so good?

Mini-Dramas

Select couples at random to act out their ideas of a good conversation on a first date. Try these both rehearsed and unrehearsed. Rehearsed conversations will demonstrate expectations; unrehearsed conversations will demonstrate the pressure involved.

Chapter Three:
THE DATING HABIT

Dating has become such a habit in our culture that much of it has become thoughtless and automatic. Thoughtlessness is next to mindlessness. As Christians, however, we need to ask ourselves why we are dating. For one thing, much dating is done for selfish motives. For another, without some imagination and selflessness, dating as an institution can really be a big bore.

Good Reasons to Date

Get to Know Someone Better. Fred and Rosie both work part-time at a department store. Each finds the other attractive and friendly. But it is a busy store, and it would be unfair to the store management if Fred hung around the cash register when he is supposed to be out on the sales floor. What is Fred to do? He doesn't want to get fired from talking to her too much. Solution? Ask her out.

When two people are attracted to each other at work, school, church, or club meeting, it is time for them to have a date together. That way, they can get to know each other without anxiety, and they can still give their full attention to their jobs, meetings, or worship services.

Fun. Larry is suffering from "tired brain." He just finished his final exams—English, chemistry, modern European history, physics, and an eight-hour take home exam in calculus—all in one week. Right now he's not even sure he ever wants to open another book again. At any rate, it's Friday and he and Renee are going roller skating tonight. *Maybe we'll get a pizza afterwards*, thinks Larry. *It'll be nice to relax my mind and coast for a change. Besides, I earned it.*

We agree. After a grueling week of school, sometimes accompanied by a constant sports program, part-time work, or who-knows-what, it is time for a little recreation and relaxation. There is certainly nothing wrong with having fun, especially when it is interspersed with a constructive and challenging work schedule. And good dates are certainly fun.

Avoid Isolation. Lizzie is smart and single. She works full-time as a forklift operator. She also lives alone. She spends much of her spare time reading, playing the guitar, and making macrame wall hangings. Recently she asked one of her co-workers over for dinner. They had a great time. Jerry was surprised to find out how intelligent and talented Lizzie is. Lizzie was just happy to be able to relate to another human being. She had spent so much time by herself.

Sometimes our social circumstances prevent us from having balanced social lives. Through the institution of dating, however, we can create our own social lives. God made people to be with people. Dating can help us to keep our balance as social creatures.

Spouse Seeking. One thing that Fred, Rosie, Larry, Renee, Lizzie, and Jerry have in common is that they are looking at their partners in light of their own values, goals, likes, dislikes, personal habits, allegiance to Christ, and general compatibility. This evaluating process theoretically gets more intense as one gets older. If you are in junior high, you don't have to ask yourself, "Could I marry this person?" There is, after all, nothing wrong with dating just for fun. But you do

reap what you sow. As you get older, the stakes in a relationship get higher; marriage increasingly invades the minds of the dating partners. Therefore, at any age, it is best to choose dating partners with care. If you do that from the beginning, then by the time you are of marriageable age, you will probably have a clear idea of the kind of person you want to settle down with. Your circle of friends will include a higher percentage of these people who would "work out."

Bad Reasons to Date

You can be sure that not everybody dates for the reasons stated above. The problem is, most of the other reasons for dating are selfish and destructive, like:

Prestige. LeMar is your average guy—middle class all the way. He doesn't look especially good. Or bad. He plays second-string on the football team. He doesn't dress with a special amount of good taste. Or bad. Freda is in a couple of his classes at school. Freda is "high class" all the way—pretty face, nice figure, nice clothes, a cheerleader. She knows and associates with all the socially elite at school. LeMar is tired of being mediocre. He would like to have some high-class friends. He figures that if he could date Freda, he would become a part of her social group. As for Freda, she probably wouldn't look twice at Mr. Average LeMar except for one thing: he drives a 1943 metallic blue Ford pickup truck which he restored and customized himself. Freda figures that she could raise *her* prestige by riding around in such a vehicle. Of course, to accomplish that, she'll have to date LeMar.

Dating for prestige is exploitation. Often people date each other because one has what the other person covets, be it prestige, money, popularity, or fancy transportation. Not only is Freda getting exploited by LeMar and vice versa, but chances are that little true human reaction will result from this relationship(?). LeMar will be looking beyond Freda to the popularity he can find in her social circle. Likewise, Freda will be too busy grooving on LeMar's truck to get to know *him.*

Cause Jealousy. Calvin is attracted to Zelda. But Zelda refuses to date him as long as he eagerly asks her two or three times per week. So Calvin has a scheme: he'll ask out Doris, very conspicuously. He knows he can get a date with Doris anytime, because she constantly flirts with him. Calvin's hope is that Zelda will notice that Cal is "hotter property" than she first thought. Then she may agree to respond to Calvin while she still has the option.

But what about Doris? To Calvin, she was a nonentity—a stepping stone to Zelda. Calvin exploited her. And suppose Zelda does get jealous and accepts a date the next time Calvin asks her? So what? She doesn't really want or like Calvin; she just wants to recover her slightly squashed ego. People begin to want what they fear they will lose.

Revenge. Frank and Flo have been going together

for eight months. Frank has decided that he's tired of Flo, so he dumps her. Even though Flo is still hung up on Frank, she accepts a date with Herbie a short week later. Not only does she accept the date, but she acts very affectionately toward her new date, and caresses and kisses Herbie in public as much as possible so that word will get back to Frank. Flo does not really feel affectionate toward Herbie; she is merely doing this to make Frank feel as though he never meant very much to her.

Sex. Missy has a nice figure. I mean, *really* nice. Heads turn wherever she walks, especially on the beach. Lanny sees Missy often at school, and he agrees: Missy has a nice figure. In fact, Lanny is just aching to get his hands on as much of Missy's figure as he can.

"Missy, how would you like to take in a dinner and a movie with me this Friday night?"

An appalling number of dates are elaborately designed and carried out with only one thing in mind: the maximum amount of physical involvement. According to traditional role playing, it has been lusty boys who try to corrupt innocent females, but it seems to work both ways.

Misery Loves Company.

BILLY: Oh, it has been so hard since the house burned down. We lost all we had. My parents are still in the hospital. I just don't know how we'll ever recover.

LOUISE: I know just what you mean. It's been just like that for us since my dad and brother drowned on that fishing trip. I miss them so much. Sob, sob, sob. Cry, cry.

BILLY: There, there. I know you'll be OK. Something

will work out just like things are getting better for us. Why, just this morning the doctor
said my dad had a 50-50 chance to live.
Choke, sob. Cry, cry, cry.

LOUISE: Oh, Billy, don't cry. One of us has to be strong.
BILLY: Yeah, sniff. Well, at least we have each other.
LOUISE: Yeah!
BOTH: Kiss, kiss, kiss. Hug, hug, hug. Smooch, smooch, smooch. OOoooh. We're so in love!
LOUISE: I'm so glad we found each other. I don't know what we'd do if we hadn't fallen in love at the right time.

They would probably have grown up. Hard times can produce intense grief. Intense emotions can masquerade as other intense emotions. Sympathy has a special talent for posing as love. What a bore—a relationship built on two people continually dumping their "bummers" on each other!

The Bad Date Common Denominator. In case you have not guessed it by now, all the wrong reasons for dating involve exploitation—that is, reducing the other person to merely a means to a desired end. The person who dates for prestige is exploiting the other person's popularity (or truck) to gain status he has not earned. Those who date to get revenge or to induce jealousy are exploiting the new partner to gain some sort of control over the other one. Dating for sex simply uses the other person as an outlet to satisfy a biological urge. And "misery loves company" partners are too grief stricken and self-centered to *love* the other person.

Breaking the Dating Habit

Sometimes the dating habit can get to be a drag. With some couples, the only week-to-week variation is *which* restaurant and *which* movie, or whether the game is played "at home" or "away." Remember the differences between spectating and participating?

Another advantage to participation dates is that you are not limited to the activities that are offered by other organizations. You can create your own activities. Here are some examples:

—**Going fishing.** It's a great opportunity to talk, the scenery is usually pleasant, and the activity gives you a good, casual opportunity to laugh and unwind.

—**Cooking a dinner.** Hey, girls! Don't sell guys short on domestic expertise. Many of them have at least one specialty they like to cook up from time to time. So have a "role reversal" night and let the guy prepare his favorite specialty for the girl. Another approach would be for the two of you to learn to prepare some special recipe together.

—**Local, natural fun spots.** Almost every town, village, or burg has at least one natural or historical site of interest nearby, yet we tend to ignore the things "in our own backyard." It would be interesting to find out how many Californians seldom go to the beach or climb the mountains, how many Floridians have never bothered to experience the Everglades, how many Kentuckians have never visited Mammoth Cave. Take a drive to the mountains, the country, the city, the river, the beach, the old graveyard, the rapids, the Indian mounds, or to whatever else is nearby.

—**Museums.** This may sound too "educational" for you, but museums are fun! And there are many kinds: art, natural history, science and industry, crafts, local personalities, halls of fame, local history, observatories and planetariums. Raise your level of awareness and have fun at the same time. Most museums are either cheap or free. Visiting a museum also allows plenty of time for the two of you to talk and to get to know each other.

—**Coloring books.** Get a good set of watercolors and/or crayons, and a coloring book of your favorite cartoon character—Dennis the Menace, Donald Duck, Peanuts, etc., and spend the evening coloring and talking. One of my favorite methods is to get Crayola's 64-color set and "go nuts." (Try coloring Dennis the Menace's overalls gold lamé and his shirt olive green.) Or use the watercolors and arrive at some subtle shades not found in the Sunday comics. It's easy to talk and color, so there should be plenty of relaxed communication on a date like this.

—**Creative writing.** If you and a friend both like to write poetry or short stories, get your portfolios together and share them with each other. Or spend an evening composing a poem or song together. Or write a play together and then produce and direct it with some friends. Write a short story together, spinning ideas off each others' minds.

—**Photography.** Grab or borrow a couple of cameras and go picture taking some pleasant (or rainy) afternoon. Try some "arty" shots, unusual compositions, and goofy poses of each other. Shoot up a roll apiece. Then get together a week later and compare the results (provided, of course, that you took the film to be developed in the meantime).

—**Shooting cans.** Get a BB gun (check with local laws and take necessary safety precautions). Set up some tin cans, and cardboard targets, and trade shots (at the targets).

—**Roller-skating.** Some people consider roller-skating standard fare. Others think it's outdated. Either way, it is still fun, even if it doesn't get the attention it did in the Fifties (and they *still* play the Hokie Pokie record every night). Skating is good exercise, massages your feet (and sometimes your seat), and is another good opportunity for conversation.

—**Handcrafting.** Find an old piece of furniture and refinish it. Collect old toys from the neighborhood, repair and repaint them, and give them to poor children. Learn to macrame plant hangers, belts, and bags. If you have access to a kiln, fashion and glaze something ceramic.

—**Ministering to the lonely.** Go to a local nursing home, old folks' home, mental hospital, orphanage, or hospital, and spend a few hours talking with some of the residents. This could easily become a regular activity.

—**Environmental improvement.** Find out where your local recycling center is. Then get some cardboard boxes and select a trashy area to clean up. Throw away the garbage litter; recycle the glass and metal.

—**Crash evangelism.** Go "cold turkey" calling together at a shopping mall, campus, or laundromat. Or make some calls together on prospective members of your church or youth group. Or just call on a friend who has "hit the pits"—somebody feeling lonely or depressed.

—And don't forget possibilities for tennis, golf, bowling, boating or canoeing, Ping-Pong, shuffleboard, tetherball, bicycling, hiking, picking wildflowers, sled riding, snowman building, and go-carting.

The above dates offer several advantages over more common dates: most of them stimulate creativity, some are educational, some are helpful to others, most are relaxing. They are not self-centered activities. All are fun; all give a couple unique and unhurried ways to get to know one another better. Most of them are also inexpensive or free. Several challenge our life-styles and attitudes. Some people may even be too inhibited to try them out, which may make some of these suggested dates unsuitable for "first-date" situations. But many people will welcome the change of pace; and involvement in these activities will certainly perk up the relationships of those who date regularly.

#3

Questions to Consider

Don't belabor questions 1 and 2 if other answers don't come readily. Questions 3—5 are particularly important for relating the custom of dating to Christianity. Question 6 could become a project. Assign a committee of three or four to formulate some ideas for healthy, church sponsored boy/girl activities.

1. Besides the ones mentioned in this chapter, what are some other good reasons to go on a date?

2. What are some other bad reasons to go on a date?

3. Is it all right to date someone for the main reason of winning him/her to Christ?

4. At what point should dating begin to be more for spouse seeking than for fun? Is there such a point?

5. Are there some specific social events at which it is a distinct advantage not to have a date? If so, what are they?

6. Should the church provide more opportunities for singles "mixers" and also for group events for creative and less selfish dates?

Projects

As this book suggests, it may be difficult for a young person to convince a prospective date to spend an evening coloring books, or an afternoon picking up trash. So for Project 1, it might be wiser to assign such dates to couples (real or fabricated) within the group. Then have each couple report how the dates went—what they felt, whether it was easy to talk to one another, etc.

Project 2 is an exercise in breaking out of the traditional sex roles assigned by our society. Where a girl may appear "forward" to ask a boy out to a restaurant or movie, somehow she can usually get by with asking him home for dinner. (Some cultures in our country may not even allow this until the couple is established.) If someone is willing to try Project 2, let her—but certainly do not make it a requirement of anyone.

In order to properly apply Project 3, it is crucial that the boy adapt the activity to the personality of the girl involved. For instance, he'll get a better response if he takes an athletic-type canoeing, an art major on a photography spree, or a studious person to a museum. Such advice is only to minimize the chance of rejection, *not* to encourage stereotyping.

1. If your group is evenly divided between boys and girls, assign couples to do one of the suggested dates in this chapter. Next week let them report the results to the rest.

2. Leftover Girls: Invite someone over (a boy) for a joint meal-cooking date.

3. Leftover Guys: Ask a girl out this week. Ask her to go with you on one of the dates suggested in this chapter.

4. Divide into five groups and have each group rank its order of preference to the following sets of dates:

Group 1	Group 2	Group 3	Group 4	Group 5
Dinner & movie	Big social event	Party	Hayride	Picnic
		Tennis	Shooting BB's	Swimming
Bowling	Sled riding	Cooking		Lecture
Pinball			Museum	
	Football game	Shopping		Golf
Coloring book or daily funnies		Basketball game	Miniature golf	Table tennis
	Concert			
			Baseball game	
	Photography			
Drive in the country				

5. Ask these same groups to take surveys among school friends. Keep separate records for Christians and non-Christians. Get together next week and compile the results.

Chapter Four:
PAIRING UP
(Going Steady)

We all tend to develop favorites. Most of us have a favorite set of clothes, a favorite car, style of house, or Bible translation. After getting into the dating habit, many individuals realize that one person stands out among the people they have dated. The favorites pair up and often begin dating each other exclusively. There are also couples who go steady simply because no one else ever gave either of them a second look. Either way, our culture has a step between dating around and engagement, called "going steady." At this stage the couple dates each other exclusively without making any claim on each other's future. They may exchange some token of exclusivity such

as high-school rings (readjusted by rubber bands or wax). But many couples claim the same exclusivity whether any metal is exchanged or not.

The "rules" of dating change when you pair up. They are basically as follows:

1. The couple has exclusive dating rights on each other. Neither is allowed to ask out or accept a date from another person during the going-steady period.

2. Since the couple has established a sense of "belonging" to each other, they usually buy each other gifts for Christmas, birthdays, Valentine's Day, and sometimes every other excuse including Autumnal Equinox and Groundhog's Day.

3. As steadies get more comfortable with each other, they do more familiar and common activities together, such as watching TV at each other's houses, washing each other's cars, and going shopping. This

practice allows the couple more time to be with each other without necessarily spending money on each other for traditional dates.

In other words, in a steady relationship, the participants quit trying to impress each other and simply start enjoying the togetherness. What does official "pairing up" have to offer?

Advantages of Going Steady

Dating Security. Today is Tuesday. Homecoming is Friday. Lisa rushes home from school and sits by the telephone all evening. Wednesday: a repeat performance. Finally, on Thursday at 8:37, the phone rings for her. Arnie Ignatz wants to take her to homecoming. Lisa wants to go to homecoming very badly, since she is a senior. Arnie is a 5'3" sophomore. His face is cluttered with scruffy peach fuzz and acne. He has yet to learn about underarm deodorant. Lisa has ten seconds to decide just how badly she wants to go to homecoming.

Flashback to Tuesday. Lisa's friend Mary is at home singing to herself. She has just made two phone calls: one to her hairdresser for an appointment Thursday afternoon; one to the florist for a yellow rose boutonniere. Yellow should go nicely with Johnny's brown tuxedo. Johnny and Mary are going steady. In fact, Mary was never asked to homecoming, either. All Johnny said was, "What color of dress are you wearing next Friday?"

Going steady offers a certain degree of security of escorts for special social events. It protects one from being dateless or "stuck" with an "undesirable" person.

Emotional Security. There is a second kind of security offered by an exclusive relationship: security that someone your own age is "on your side." Sometimes our world seems to be crashing down on us. Adults yell at us and often do not try to understand; little brothers and sisters try our patience; even our own

44

friends may ridicule or gossip about us. Through the thick of the conflict, a steady partner can be a good listener who tries to understand and not condemn.

Meaningful Affection. In a steady relationship, affectionate actions are more often the result of affectionate feelings. Kisses and caresses mean something. They symbolize trust, attraction, and some degree of commitment. The same kisses in a "dating around" situation are much more casual in significance.

Builds Self-esteem. Trish never liked herself very much. She is the second of three children. Her elder brother always received much praise and attention from her parents because he is their firstborn son. Likewise, her little sister gets large doses of cuddling and cooing because she is "the baby of the family." Trish feels as though she got lost in the shuffle. Consequently, when Larry started taking her out, and later asked her to go steady, she hardly knew what to think. No one had taken that much notice of her before. Larry has made her feel worthwhile. She now knows that she is likeable, which in turn has boosted Trish's self-confidence. She is no longer hesitant to speak up or offer help to people in need.

Knowing that someone likes you more than anyone else can work wonders for your self-esteem. A balanced self-esteem is important for becoming a loving and giving person.

Saves Money (maybe). "Better is a dish of vegetables where love is, than a fattened ox and hatred with it" (Proverbs 15:17, NASB). Going steady can save money in the dating process. Familiarity and acceptance allow couples to plan activities for the mere sake of togetherness. They no longer feel a great urge to try to impress each other with a display of "bucks." Have a dish of vegetables with someone you love.

Teaches the Value of Relationships. Six months ago you would not have liked Laurie. She is an only child, "spoiled rotten." She was so detached from her peers that she could say the cruelest things to them without realizing it. Since she had never experienced true friendship or closeness (her parents always showed their love through a shower of consumer goods), she was entirely ignorant of the attitude and actions necessary for fostering and maintaining relationships. Then Jerry started coming over to see her. Laurie considered Jerry strange at first because he said he liked her, but he never gave her presents. He would sit and let her rattle on about herself for a while, but then he would say, "Now it's my turn." Or he would take her to a meadow to pick wildflowers, or to a museum or the zoo. Laurie began to notice the power of her words and responses. She could make Jerry feel glad or sad, depending on the way she talked and acted. Evidently Laurie was changing, because whenever she hurt Jerry's feelings, she felt just awful inside. Soon this attitude began to affect her relationships with other people. She began to listen instead of talking all the time. Before she spoke, she tried to think about how someone would react. Before she and Jerry had started dating, she had never known what it was to place value on another human being.

A major advantage of a steady relationship is that it can teach you about the nature of human relationships. Laurie is an extreme case to illustrate a point, but the principle holds true. The closer you get to someone, the less selfish you can remain if you want to be happy. Once the concept of selflessness is learned, it can apply to other areas of one's life. Jerry taught Laurie the value of relationships, starting with *step one.* But at whatever the stage, a steady relationship can teach us *something* about getting along with people in the wider areas of our social life.

On the Other Hand

Going steady is like a bed of roses. Those were the blossoms; now for the thorns. Heavy relationships can also be an unnecessary burden, especially if you try to mean too much to each other too soon. Going steady prematurely brings with it its own brand of special temptations which can seriously attack your relationship to Christ and your responsibility to grow. The greatest problems arise from going steady when you are too young or immature in personal, emotional, and social development.

Identity Problems. What is Patty like? Right now, she likes to watch hockey games, eat a lot of pizza, and listen to Tina Turner records. Her favorite color is orange. Her hair is layered, she wears false eyelashes, and she recently had her ears pierced. She wears tennis shoes and jogging suits. Patty's current boyfriend is George. George plays hockey, eats at least three pizzas per week, and is a Turner fan. His team color is orange. He is attracted to girls who have layered hair, long eyelashes, pierced ears, and who wear tennis shoes and jogging suits.

Last year, Patty liked basketball, yogurt, bran, grapefruit, and Cyndi Lauper. She had a curly permanent. She thought false eyelashes were "dumb" and pierced ears unhealthy. She let only natural brand shoes touch her feet as she habitually slipped into denim jumpsuits or overalls. Larry, her boyfriend at the time, played basketball, preferred Cyndi Lauper music, and curly hair. He preferred the "natural" life-style, which accounted for Patty's unpierced ears, lack of makeup, her natural shoes and clothes, and organic diet.

What is Patty like? She is a carbon copy in preferences and personality to her current boyfriend. Patty has changed personalities two or three times per year

ever since she first started going steady with someone at age twelve. Between boyfriends she is moody, sullen, quiet, and sits in her room and watches TV. She doesn't know what to do with herself.

If going steady becomes a habit and way of life at too early an age, it can bring with it a *false* security in which your boy/girl friend becomes your identity. No true personality of your own has a chance to develop. Then when you are left alone, all you find is boredom and frustration within yourself.

Getting Hot and Heavy. "Tsk, tsk. My, my. Julie's pregnant. I just don't understand it. She and Joe were such nice kids."

That is the whole point. It is the nice kids who get "caught" because they never intended to "go all the way" in the first place. If they had not been "nice kids," they probably would have taken some precautions for their "roll in the hay." But for Joe and Julie to buy some sort of birth control beforehand would have meant that they intended to disobey God all along.

So here is another disadvantage of going steady. If you get too close emotionally to someone, your body will want to follow (sometimes it leads). Pacing a steady relationship can be difficult, especially if you are years away from a feasible marriageable age. Many times Christian couples fall into premarital sex simply as a result of a close relationship. The fact that they "fall into" sexual intercourse also means that they are unprepared for birth control. That, in turn, means that not only are they sinning, they are playing with life forces. There is no easy repentance for a premarital pregnancy.

Another disadvantage of premarital sex is that it is the expression of the "two becoming one flesh" without it happening in actuality. It is like signing your name to a book that you did not write. Premarital intercourse is living a lie, because you are not truly living as one. That can happen only in marriage.

Of course, the strongest reasons for abstaining from premarital sex are the myriad of commands in the Bible. Since God invented sex, He knows best how it should be handled for ultimate maximum enjoyment. There are so many verses, in fact, that most Christian books about dating spend most of their space on this subject, probably because it is the only part of dating that has so much information in the Bible. Rather than reiterate what all the other books say, here is a list of pertinent verses for you to study on your own: Acts 15:20, 29; 21:25; Romans 1:29; 1 Corinthians 5:1; 6:9, 13, 18; 7:2; 2 Corinthians 12:21; Galatians 5:19; Ephesians 5:3; Colossians 3:5; 1 Thessalonians 4:3. You may want to look up *fornication* in the dictionary first.

In the meantime, how do you handle these intense feelings, especially if you are going steady? First Corinthians 6:18 tells us to "Flee from sexual immorality" (NIV). Paul recognizes in this verse that the sex drive is very strong. *We* should not test our ability to resist—it will be tested enough without our adding to it. Rather, we should avoid situations that have potential for sexual temptation. Don't give yourselves long, private time periods together. It also means that both of you should get out of the car as soon as the motor is stopped. Parking, arranging to be home when your parents are out, and secretly meeting together alone are not ways to *flee* sexual immorality. Don't compromise with the ways of the world!

Resisting temptation will build your character as individuals and as a couple. Your respect for yourselves and for each other will increase. And you will not be carrying the dual burdens of guilt and possible pregnancy which haunt so many steady couples the morning after they "do it."

So, What's Next? Now that you're going steady, what is the next step? Do you assume that you will break up? Or do you plan to get engaged (or preengaged) and then married? There are no immediately attractive answers if you're in junior high or high school. Breaking up is no fun, and engagement and marriage before graduation from high school is scary at best. Can you continue as steadies indefinitely? How does a couple build a relationship without thinking of marriage? How does a couple stop thinking about marriage without breaking up? Many times couples panic when they realize that they are very close to one another and yet are years away from a workable marriage. They don't want to get married yet, they don't want to wait for sex, and they don't want to break up. So they continue in a relationship that offers some social advantages but no basic purpose or direction.

The Trap. Jack is sixteen, a junior in high school. He has been going steady with Debbie for six months. Sometimes they have even talked about the possibility of getting married "when they are old enough." Lately, however, the normally sweet and congenial Debbie has been grouchy and domineering. Not only that, but there is a very attractive and friendly girl named Brenda at church who evidently likes Jack, too. Jack now feels trapped against his will. Soon he is taking Brenda out. "After all," justifies Jack, "I'm only sixteen. Why should I be tied down at such a young age?"

This is one reason that fights and unfaithfulness often accompany "steady" relationships. Sometimes there is simply not enough reason to stay together in the face of the difficulties of growing up.

Curtains. "Breaking up is hard to do." Breaking up is often so unpleasant, in fact, that the fears of tears, anger, hostility, and guilt can keep a couple together when split-up time is long past due. Some couples even get married more out of fear of being alone than out of love for and commitment to each other. So going steady usually means someday you are going to have to break up. And "breaking up is hard to do."

How to Go Steady (and stay Christian)

Going steady is neither right nor wrong within itself. The main disadvantages occur when you try to go steady before you are mature enough to handle a one-to-one relationship. How you handle your own particular relationship will determine whether going steady is a good or bad thing for you. And, of course, the best and most growth-provoking relationships will be based on the words of Christ and the apostles. There are lessons to be learned about romance in the "love Chapter," 1 Corinthians 13. Admittedly, the primary context of this chapter concerns the attitude to be used in administering one's spiritual gifts. Furthermore, Paul does not *define* love, but he does a great job *describing* it. Even so, when Christlike love becomes the goal of steady couples, their relationships take on some exciting dimensions. Psychologists and sociologists have often cited the attitudes that make for long-lived, well-balanced relationships; the same principles can be derived from 1 Corinthians 13:4-7.

Love is:

Patient. It lets the other person grow up on his own instead of trying to do the growing up for him. This is an attitude of *active* patience, rather than a teeth-grating "When's he gonna stop?" tolerance.

Kind. Love has a gentle, favorable, and optimistic attitude toward the other person. This attitude is characterized by gentle and understanding actions.

Not Envious. Rather, it rejoices in the blessings of the loved one. Love has no mind for exploitation.

Not Boastful or Proud. A true lover is not preoccupied with his own self-importance. His ego is not excessively fed by the fact that 1) he has an ability to love; 2) he is lovable; 3) his partner is attractive or desirable. Nor does he act in a superior or condescending manner to the loved one.

Not Rude. The positive opposite to this is "Love is polite." Love does not take the other person for granted. One reason marriages and romances go stale is that neither partner bothers to try to make the other person feel special anymore. Politeness is making someone feel special.

Not Self-seeking. It is *other-person* seeking. Each enters the relationship thinking of what he can give, rather than get. Each will be more preoccupied with the other person's successes, blessings, hurts, mistakes, and encounters than with his own.

Slow to Anger. In addition, the anger of true love rises when the loved one is hurting *himself*. It is not merely guided by one's own comfort level. Disagreements can be discussed without immediately degenerating into irrational arguments.

Love also:

Keeps No Record of Wrongs. This is an important element in being able to disagree constructively. Love forgives *and* forgets. It does not dig up dead and buried mistakes in order to shame the partner. This also means that love confronts one conflict at a time, rather than letting a batch of them accumulate for emotional ammunition. It does not assume unspoken expectations and then pout when they are unfulfilled by the partner.

Rejoices in Truth. "Truth" is the way things really are. "Rejoicing" means being happy. Therefore, love is happy with the way things really are. In other words, love accepts the other person as he or she really is. To try to change a person from what he/she is, is to love a theoretical ideal rather than the real flesh-and-blood person.

Protects. The loved one is special. The lover tries to understand his partner and has a desire to protect the other from physical or emotional damage. Love builds up the other person. Sincere affirmations of the other person's worth will help protect him from a misunderstanding and hostile world.

Trusts. Love does not attempt to supervise every thought and action of the other person. It respects his identity. Love believes the best in the other person even when there may be a lack of understanding.

Hopes. Suppose you are looking through a telescope. At first, all you see is a rubbish heap. Then you change the focus without moving the instrument. Suddenly a beautiful garden pops into focus while the junk pile becomes a blur. The hope aspects of love are like that. Love is not *blind* to the faults of the other person, but the *focus*—the emphasis—is on the beautiful aspects of the other person. This helps those characteristics to grow until there is no room left for the rubbish.

Perseveres. Love does not give up when it encounters obstacles such as communication breakdowns, unexpected or erratic behavior, momentary insults, and walkouts. That does not mean that perseverent love is a doormat. Sometimes it is necessary to love someone from a distance to help the other person grow and appreciate relationships.

It would take a lot of maturity to practice the kind of love that 1 Corinthians 13:4-7 describes. In fact, *very few married* couples demonstrate that kind of love. But if you want a marriage later that is characterized by mature love, now is the time to start letting these principles guide you in your encounters with your boy/girl friend, parents, family, and other friends, because God's love takes a lifetime to grow into.

Putting Your Closeness to Work

—"Carry each other's burdens, and in this way you will fulfill the law of Christ" (Galatians 6:2, NIV).
—"Therefore confess your sins to each other and pray for each other so you may be healed" (James 5:16, NIV).
—"Bear with each other and forgive whatever grievances you may have against one another.... Let the word of Christ dwell in you richly as you teach and admonish one another with all wisdom, and as you sing psalms, hymns, and spiritual songs with gratitude in your hearts to God" (Colossians 3:13, 16, NIV).

Has it ever occurred to you that these verses can apply to Christians who are going steady? Maybe you are too afraid to "confess your sins" to the guy sitting next to you in your church pew. You feel uneasy about the thought of teaching and counseling the kid that sits across from you at Sunday school, especially since he never asked you to. So why not start with your boyfriend or girl friend? (This is one reason it is smart to let yourself get serious only with other Christians.) Here are some ways to put your steady relationship to work to bring about active, positive spiritual growth in both of your lives.

Count Your Blessings—Together! First of all, realize that God is working in your lives. Think about the ways God has made your life better. Then get together to share the spiritual victories each of you has had that week. Did a friend accept Christ recently? Did you finally say something nice to your parents?

Did God give you strength to meet a special task, a chronic temptation, or a difficult trial? Surely something has happened this week! Telling each other about the victories will give you a more positive attitude about being a Christian, and it will help you to realize the constant care that God has been giving you all along.

Get Into the Word. The real stability and "meat" of your Christian lives will be supplied by the Word of God. The Scriptures have a way of ministering to whatever deficiencies we may have as individuals. For example, when an egotistical person reads the Bible, he is overwhelmed by God's greatness and power; his own inflated self-opinion shrinks in response. When the timid self-rejecting person opens the Word of God, the unequivocal love which the Father offers there can change him. The procrastinator comes to a better understanding of the importance of others and of commitments. The selfish person is confronted in the Book by the blessings he already has and by the needs of others around him.

What the Bible can do for individuals it can do for romantic couples. Together, pick out a passage, chapter, or book from the Bible, but read it individually. Then get together again and discuss the ways that this particular passage affects your lives as individuals and as a couple.

Bear Each Other's Burdens. All of us succumb to temptation from time to time. We fail in things we set out to do. We are overwhelmed by circumstances. A Christian couple should share these defeats with each other, provided they keep these points in mind:

—Never use another's admitted failures as a lever to beat him in an argument, to shame him, or to gain power over him.

—Remember that the purpose of sharing bad experiences is to defeat the problem, not to bask in it.

—Turn all your problems over to God's power from the beginning. The first purpose of prayer is not to

make the problem to go away; it is to admit complete dependence upon God's power and mercy.

—Discern the difference between a "burden" and the "main load" (Galatians 6:2, 5, NIV). We are obligated as Christians to lessen the trials that each of us receives, but we are NOT allowed to live someone else's life for him.

—Do not dwell overly long on the negative aspects of your lives, or your romance may turn into a "misery-loves-company" setup.

As you pray for one another, a word of caution is in order: It is particularly healthy for the two of you to pray for each other when you are apart. Care should be taken if you decide to pray together, however. Many engaged Christian couples have fallen into premarital sex after an intense prayer session together. The spiritual and emotional closeness that results from a long, heartfelt private prayer session together often brings about a fierce desire for physical closeness as well. Pray for each other at home. You may even want to set up a certain time each day to pray for each other when you are apart. It helps your self-image to know that someone somewhere is praying just for you. Of course, the fact is secondary to the knowledge that two children of God are talking to the Lord of the universe about the same things at the same time.

#4

Questions to Consider

1. Should a person make an effort to go steady with someone he/she has been dating?

2. What is a good age to start going steady? Should parents decide on the age and then enforce it upon their children?

3. Should you go steady even if you know you will break up later? If so, why?

4. Is it all right to go steady with a non-Christian? Why or why not?

5. How closely is going steady tied to engagement?

6. If a person has been "dating around" for a few years, is there a stage at which he/she should begin to think about going steady? For instance, if a twenty-year-old has been dating since he/she was fifteen, and has never gone steady, do you think that person might be too "picky" or noncommittal?

Projects

1. Read the book of Proverbs. Note the verses which best apply to dating or going steady. Have those involved share their favorite verses and explain how they relate to dating.

Or, assign a few of these verses to different people in the group (or as small group projects). Have them report their findings to the group at large. The purpose of this project is to relate the mind of God more specifically to the practical aspects of dating. The most pertinent verses are Proverbs 10:12, 17; 11:3-5, 12, 17; 12:15, 18, 23; 13:2; 14:10, 15, 30; 15:1, 4, 17, 18, 23, 28, 30; 16:1, 17, 24, 28, 32; 17:27; 18:13; 19:11; 20:22; 21:2; 24:10, 17; 25:11, 15, 17, 28; 26:17; 27:4, 5; 30:18, 19, 21-23; 31:10.

2. Select a steady couple from your group (if you have one). Have them enact a dinner date:

        a. as it was.
        b. as they do now as a steady couple.
   3. Have them simulate going for a walk or a drive:
        a. as they did.
        b. as they do now.
   4. Have the boy ask out his girl friend:
        a. as he did the first time.
        b. as he does now.

Chapter Five:
BREAKING UP

How morbid! Devoting 20% of the study to such a negative topic as "breaking up."

"But I wanted to learn about how to date, not how to end it."

But dating is usually a cycle: dating around, going steady, breaking up, dating around . . . and on and on until one of the "steadies" becomes an engagement, and then (if you're lucky) the engagement becomes a marriage. So, except for the one you marry, you will break up every time you go steady. There are hundreds of Christian books about dating, going steady, engagement and marriage. But what about when you get "dumped," or have to dump someone else? Even engagements have a 50% failure rate. That is when it is hardest to be Christlike. Since breaking up is part of the dating cycle, let's learn how to do it right.

The Seven Warning Signs of a Cancerous Relationship

There are times when it is much healthier to break up than to stay together. Often we are so wrapped up in the relationship that we refuse to see the "danger signals" that may be wrecking our futures, our personhoods, and our relationships to Christ. There are, however, at least seven danger signs that can let us recognize when our emotional dependence has superseded our common sense.

I. Fighting to Extreme

A few fights are healthy. In fact, a close couple who *never* fight are evidently not interacting. A couple can also fight too much. Certainly, if your fights outnumber, outlast, or equal your peace times, that is too much. Occasionally over a period of a few days to a week, even a "good" couple may mostly fight, but the time to worry is when fights, loud disagreements, and emotion-filled arguing fill your time together over a period of weeks and months.

II. Too Much Physical Involvement

FRED: Hi.
CHERYL: Hi.
FRED: [silence]
CHERYL: [silence]
FRED: Let's make out!
CHERYL: Yeah, O.K.!

Fred and Cheryl illustrate the sum total of some couples' relationships: no stimulating or challenging activities, no conversation, no communication. Just a purely physical relationship—which isn't the same as a physically pure relationship. It is one thing for physical attraction to help start a relationship. It is another thing to *gratify* that relationship from the first date forward. When that happens, there is nowhere for the relationship to go. Couples who are stuck at this stage should break up. They will get (or already are) bored and frustrated with each other, which feels even worse than feeling lonely when in solitude.

Sometimes a relationship starts out well balanced, but winds down to nothing but hugging, kissing, and petting. Whichever way a couple gets stuck at this stage, they should back off and evaluate the total relationship. If there is nothing other than the physical relationship, they should break up before they bore each other to death!

And while we're on the subject, remember that premarital *intercourse* is wrong, whether it is a little or a lot. God does not prohibit sex outside of marriage to spoil our fun. One reason God does prohibit it is that it is contrary to the system of love and marriage that He designed. Anything we consistently do which is contrary to God's design will eventually destroy us. It would be better for us to destroy a relationship than for the relationship to destroy *us*.

III. Conflicting Goals and Values

SCENE: *A marriage counselor's office.*

COUNSELOR: I think you two had better work out your conflicting goals and value systems together before (or if) you get married.

GROOM-TO-BE: What do you mean, conflicting values? We both like poetry, pet hamsters, painting, bicycling, backgammon, and baseball.

COUNSELOR: That's not what I mean. You can have identical *interests* and still have diametrically opposed *values* or life goals.

BRIDE-TO-BE: What do you mean?

COUNSELOR: Common interests show only how compatible you will be in your *free* time. Goals and values determine who you are and what you will become for the rest of your lives. Jim, you say that two years of technical training is all the schooling you'll ever want. But Liz wants to get her doctorate in chemistry. Will you be willing to pour that much of your earnings into something you do not value highly? Liz also indicates that she would like to have you around a lot. How will you resolve that if you become a transcontinental truck driver—play backgammon over the phone?

When two lives are determined to go separate ways, the sooner the breakup, the less pain there is and the less chance there is of either person compromising his/her identity. Jim and Liz's romance started innocently enough in high school. They really did figure that they were made for each other. After all, how many people do *you* know who like both hamsters and backgammon? Their common interests made for an extraordinary dating life. But four years later when they were considering marriage, they began to realize that to stay together might shatter their hopes and dreams for life. Maybe Jim and Liz will be able to work out their differences; maybe not. The desire for companionship and love often supersedes personal goals and values. Sometimes these goals are expendable.

One value is *not* expendable for the sake of companionship—your relationship to Jesus Christ. To get emotionally involved with a non- or anti-Christian is literally "courting trouble."

"But I love him!"

Just because you have the capability to fall in love with a non-Christian does not make it God's will to do so. God's stated will is that Christians "not be yoked together with unbelievers" (2 Corinthians 6:14, NIV). Christians finding themselves involved romantically with non-Christians have an obligation to their Lord to state these obligations and allegiances to their lovers. Perhaps a solution can be worked out between a Christian and non-Christian, but not through the Christian's compromising his faith. Christians "live and move and have their being" through Christ. How close can you draw, how intimately can you share, with someone who does not even exist for the same reason you do?

IV. Abuse

Dear Gabby,

Jerry and I have been dating steadily for seven months now. Jerry is funny and handsome and I love him, but there is just one thing. He seems to enjoy hurting me. He is forever poking, pinching, and hitting me. When I tell him to stop, he just laughs.

And when we get into a fight, boy, watch out! The last time, he twisted my arm and punched my shoulder. I had a bruise for three weeks. Other times he cries and says he's sorry, and he looks like such a helpless little lamb I believe him. But in a day or two he's back at it again.

Otherwise, he's really neat, and like I said, I really love him. What should I do?

Black & Blue

Have you ever read a similar letter in an advice column? The answer is invariably the same: Break up at once; this guy is sick. He wants somebody to abuse. He may even need mental help. Or maybe he is just too immature to handle a close relationship. Either way, he doesn't deserve a girl friend. It is one thing to get teased and tickled in fun and perhaps carry it a bit too far by accident. It is quite another matter to become a human punching bag.

There is another kind of abuse that deserves mention—mental abuse. This kind is performed by either sex. It can take the form of verbal abuse (yelling, swearing, unreasonable accusations), intentional public embarrassment (making you look like a fool in front of your friends), or any number of other "mind games" your partner may play on you (lying, acting alternately "hot" and "cold," flirting with others to make you jealous). Abuse is abuse, mental or physical. To suffer silently is to reinforce the abuser's behavior.

V. Withdrawal

BOB: I wonder what's wrong with Norbie?

JOHN: Why, what do you mean?

BOB: Well, he's never around anymore. We've been his best friends. He never talks to us anymore. I hardly ever see him. I think he's quit football, too.

JOHN: Yeah. I heard that his grades are dropping badly, too. Come to think of it, he doesn't come to Bible study or Sunday school anymore.

BOB: Yeah—all he does is come to church and sit with Marsha and whisper and hold hands.

JOHN: I wonder if that's it.

BOB: Marsha?

JOHN: Has he tossed the rest of his life out the win-

63

dow—sports, school, friends, church activity, for Marsha? She's a nice girl, but isn't that carrying it a little too far?

Yes. Love "is not rude, it is not self-seeking" (1 Corinthians 13:5 NIV). True love should expand our friendships, not take them away. Love is a constructive force. It causes us to be the best persons we can be. Infatuation and mindless dependence produce dropouts from life. Relationships that crowd other friends, accomplishments, and the Lord out of our lives should be cooled or terminated.

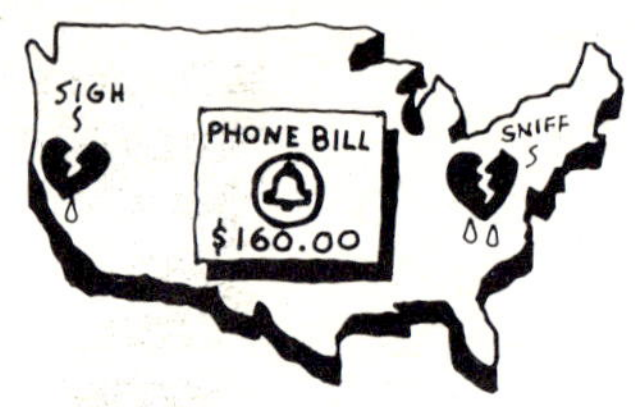

VI. Geographical Separation

Whether geographical separation should be a factor in breaking up is dependent upon two factors: the age of the "lovers," and the distance between them. For 13-14 year olds, ten miles may be enough to cool a romance. At the other extreme, engaged couples may be able to keep things alive when separated by thousands of miles. Even so, it is no "picnic" to love someone who lives far away. If one member of a steady couple moves away, there is little sense in two mid-teenagers prolonging the pain of a geographical separation by swearing to be faithful to each other, racking up horrendous long-distance phone bills, writing long letters every day, and, in general, forsaking the life the Lord has given them "here and now." It never lasts anyway unless you are older and engaged, and even then, the mortality rate on such relationships is high. Emotional dependence does not equal commitment.

VII. Bad Combination

Personalities are like chemicals. Hydrogen (a very explosive gas) and oxygen (a gas necessary for combustion) combine to form water, which puts out fires and quenches thirst. Add another oxygen atom to each molecule and you get hydrogen peroxide, which bleaches your hair and would bubble you to death if you tried to drink it.

Human relationships involve the "chemistry" of personalities. Two "dishrag" personalities *may* get together and form a "dynamic duo." Two "model citizens" in combination may become a "gruesome twosome." If two individuals' generosity, sense of humor, and peaceableness turn to selfishness, bitterness, and cynicism as a couple, they should not *be* a couple. The question for a couple to ask themselves is, "Am I better or worse for knowing and being with this person?"

A Warning Sign That Isn't One

One of the main causes of breakups is that one person gets "tired of" the other. But what does that mean? What person can excite another 100% of the time? If the relationship seems stale, sit it out. Change the pace. See what can be done to make it interesting. Even if the romance does not work out, at least you will be learning the meaning of commitment. Marriages are built on commitment, not excitement. If you get into the habit of "baling out" whenever the relationship is "stale," you may be looking for a perfect person who does not exist.

The Ineptness/Pain Ratio. Breaking up is a negative experience. It is undesirable, painful, and just plain "icky." As such, we avoid it as a topic, and consequently never learn how to break up "right." Much of the pain involved in breaking up is in direct proportion to our ineptness in going about it. Henceforth in this study, the one who initiated the breakup will be called the *"breaker."* The lover who gets unpleasantly surprised will be called the *breakee."*

Common Breaker Blunders

The Silent Treatment. Bill and Erma had been going steady for five months. In fact, the relationship seemed to be getting pretty "solid." Then one day Bill went to meet Erma at her locker for their ususal morning walk around the halls. When he arrived, Erma was already with a bunch of her girl friends, walking down the hall together, talking and laughing. Bill tried to join in, but Erma and the rest of the girls just continued to talk, ignoring his attempted interruptions. By the end of the week, Bill realized that Erma was not just having an "off day." It's all over. But Bill still does not know why Erma dropped him—she acts as if she has never seen Bill in her life. No explanation, no argument (what's a breakup without a good argument?), no apology, no announcement, nothing. As a result, Bill's mind is confused:

"Is it my fault? What did I do wrong? Is it something I said the night before? Something I did? Has Erma been putting up with me all along and just couldn't stand it anymore? Maybe I'm icky."

At other times, his thought pattern is: "What a witch! I've been good to her all along. I try to understand her, put up with all her dumb ideas, take her out and spend money on her. Last week she told me she loved me. Now she acts like I don't exist. Maybe I ought to tell her off in front of her friends. Cause a real scene. Let her know how I feel."

Of course, Erma's story is:

"I just got tired of going steady with him. I didn't know how to tell him. I wouldn't want to hurt his feelings."

Too late, Erma. Bill is already hurt, thanks to your cowardice. Were you really too "kind" to tell him or were you merely protecting your own guilt feelings? In the meantime, Bill's self-doubt could take months to heal.

Sugar-coated Reasoning. Even when the breaker tries to explain the situation to the breakee, he/she may give only surface reasons. While *emotions* usually motivate, we like to think of ourselves as noble, *rational* creatures. So the breaker may cite lofty, selfless reasons to the breakee, while selfish reasons really moved him/her to the split. For instance:

When the breaker says:	**It probably means:**
"At our age we need to be free."	"I've got another chick on the side who gives me a bigger thrill."
"We're growing in different directions."	"I don't think I'm good enough for you."
"We don't have much in common."	"You bore me; I'm tired of you."
"We don't communicate well."	"You're dumb."
"I'm going away to school."	"I don't want my fun spoiled by somebody I can't see."
"I guess I'm not ready to settle down."	"You're trying to run my life. Bug off!"
"I'm too busy for a boy/girl friend right now."	"I don't want you very badly."

If a person feels like breaking off a relationship, he should examine his/her motives and express them honestly.

Guilt Projection. Now that Jorjette is tired of Larry, she knows that it is time to break up. Of course she feels guilty about the thought of hurting him, but soon she begins rationalizing to herself.

"Why am I feeling so bad? After all, he's the one who talks too much. He wears red tennis shoes all the time, he kisses sloppy, he eats too much, laughs weird, he doesn't get his hair cut right. Sometimes I even wonder if he's as close to God as I am."

This mental process continues until Jorjette, rather than feeling guilty about dropping Larry, wonders how she ever got involved with him in the first place. She now looks forward to "telling him off." When Jorjette finally tells Larry why she's breaking up, she unloads all these negative feelings on him. Larry is crushed. Not only has he been "dumped," he has been informed that he is a totally unlikable person.

Actually, Larry is an average guy who makes an average number of mistakes. To justify dropping Larry on a whim, Jorjette has dredged up every negative thing she could possibly remember about Larry and dumped the mess on him all at once. "And you have the nerve to wonder why I'm breaking off the relationship," exhorts Jorjette.

Erratic Behavior. Barry is in a fix. He has decided that he is tired of Linda and wants to break up. But other times he is not sure if he should. Most of his actions toward Linda have grown cold—he seldom calls her, and when he does talk to her, he is cold and harsh. He never holds her hand when they walk anymore. His kisses are automatic and unfeeling. Occasionally, however, he does show a burst of enthusiasm; he "treats her like a lady"—opens doors for her, laughs at her jokes, and generates warmth and affection toward her.

To put it mildly, Linda is confused. When Barry comes to see her, she wonders, "What's going to happen this time? Is he going to drop me for good? Is this relationship going to get better? Or nothing?"

Evidently, the relationship really *is* over. The problems are: 1) Barry is not "in love" with Linda anymore, but he does not want to lose the security of a steady relationship; 2) Barry feels bad about getting tired of Linda. When he treats her like a lady, he is trying to convince himself that he still likes her. Either way, no one should indulge in the other person's patience while he makes up his mind. Serious doubt, fears, or loss of interest should be voiced when they occur.

The Meanest Way. Norma has been going steady with Jack for three months. In the last three weeks, however, she has become interested in somebody else, Maurice. Now Norma is ready to dump Jack in order to go steady with Maurice. Norma said, "I don't know how to tell Jack, and I wouldn't want to hurt him." So, in order to help Jack "get the message," Norma decided to walk around the school halls (where they all go to high school) holding hands and kissing with Maurice, making sure Jack would see them.

Jack "got the message," but I can't repeat his reaction here.

It's Not One-Sided (*Breakee Blunders*)

OK. We've just looked at all the nasty mistakes those mean ol' breakers make, but breakees aren't exempt from wrongdoing either. In fact, since they are the ones put under unexpected stress, they often express their anger and grief in ways that do not honor Christ.

Slander. Love and infatuation are strong emotions. When a person has generated much positive energy toward another, it is easier to change the sentiment than the intensity of it. That is why Suzie's "love" has turned to hate, scorn, and slander within a day of George's dumping her.

"George is such a bozo," she rails to her friends. "He picks his nose and doesn't know the first thing about eating out. I remember when he wore brown shoes with a tuxedo. And I've been so good to him and now he drops me for no reason! I don't see how anybody in her right mind would want to go out with him now."

The rationalizations behind the slander include: 1) "Even though he dumped me, he's the one who is stupid—*I'm* certainly not undesirable;" 2) "If I can't have him, neither can anyone else, at least not if *my* word gets around;" 3) "Since I can't love him, I might as well hate him." Of course, few people *verbalize* these thoughts, even to themselves, but the unconscious motivations are certainly real enough. They are *emotional,* not *logical* responses.

Guilt Induction. This is another, more direct form of revenge:

JIM: ... So anyway, I think we should break up.

LYN: Well, I'm not surprised. You never knew what responsibility was, anyway. Just go ahead and leave me. You've already hurt me every other possible way; I guess this is the only way you had left. And after the way I've loved you!

It is obvious that Lyn wants Jim to feel as bad for dumping her as she does for getting rejected.

"Just Friends." When Laura dropped Jim, he asked

her if they could still be "good friends." "After all," he reasoned, "we've gone together for seven months. Just because we've broken up doesn't mean it should ruin a good friendship." So Laura agreed.

In the last few weeks, however, Jim's definition of "good friends" has been expanding. At first, he just talked to her at school as he would anyone else. Soon, though, the conversations got longer and "friendlier." He began calling her at night on the phone, and soon after, was coming over to her house to watch TV again. "After all," he reasoned, "aren't those the things that 'good friends' do together?" Then he asked her out to dinner and a movie. Not wanting to hurt their "friendship," Laura consented. But when Jim drove her home after the date and asked, "How 'bout a kiss for a good friend?" Laura knew that Jim's game of self-deception had gone too far. She had to drop him all over again, and Jim hurt more from this second break than he did from the first. But it was his own doing. He had "set himself up" for rejection. Emotions left over from a romance are usually too intense to "gear down" immediately to merely friendly proportions. It is better to keep your contact to a minimum at least until all those funny twinges in the stomach no longer occur.

Threats, Violence, Getting High, and Co. Sometimes a breakee's reactions are so intense, they have to be labeled *sins* rather than just "mistakes." One of these is revenge in the form of threats, blackmail, or violence. Men and boys have been known to beat up girls (or at least try to) who drop them. Other times, the breakee threatens to (or does) tell others of personal secrets they had shared while going steady. Also, many people get drunk or "high" at the time they get dumped. Turning to alcohol or drugs during a crisis is a quick road to psychological dependence on the stuff; it also denies God the opportunity to heal your wounded soul. Furthermore, drunkenness is soundly condemned in the Bible (1 Corinthians 6:10; Romans 13:13; Galatians 5:21).

By "and Co.," I mean illicit sex. Many times, breakees will immediately seek casual (but intense) sex relations after a broken romance. It is usually done as a mental revenge on the "breaker," and as a compensation for the lost love.

Bounce-back Romance. After Jim saw that he could no longer ask Laura out, he began to look for somebody else who could fill the void. First, he began to talk to Clara as a "good friend" who would "understand" his hurt and loneliness. Then he began to play on her sympathies, explaining how that "mean ol' Laura" had dumped him "for no reason at all." Soon Jim and Clara were going out, and within two weeks they were going steady.

Such relationships are phony to the core. Jim never really got to know Clara at all. The relationship became very physical very quickly. Clara was just a substitute. She was being used and did not know it. Jim did not realize it either until the whole romance burnt out after three more weeks of sympathy and "making out."

Positive Ways to
Handle a Breakup

OK! That is enough about mistakes. Here are some positive things to do in a breakup (if you feel one coming on), based on Christian principles. They should help reduce some of the confusion, if not the pain, and turn a breakup into a real opportunity to grow. This advice is based on the assumption that breakups *do* hurt.

Ephesians 4:15 is a key verse for forming the right attitude in breaking off a relationship: *Speak the truth in love.* First it is important that you are truthful and honest with your former partner. Be honest with yourself as well. Do not, however, be *brutally* honest. That is where the love mentioned in Ephesians 4:15

tempers the truth you speak. Truths spoken out of jealously, anger, revenge, or any other form of ungodliness are hypocritical. As tired as you may be of the relationship, give your poor "ex" a break, and be nice.

Advice to Breakers

Instill a Sense of Worth. Remember that your former partner is taking a major loss on his/her self-esteem (the person closest to him has decided to reject him). Do not dredge up bad experiences out of the past to make him/her feel bad. The breakee feels bad enough already. Emphasize the inherent worth of the *person*, and the unfeasibility of the *relationship.*

Don't Play Games. As soon as you have a reasonable idea that you want to end the relationship, let the other person know. "Letting on" that things are OK just frustrates you and stores up an extra dose of pain for later.

Admit Your Own Mistakes. Some people bring out the worst in each other, but that does not mean that they are bad in themselves. If you have been a poor judge of character or personality chemistry, admit your mistake, at least to yourself. This should help prevent you from telling the breakee that he or she went bad or changed.

Face Reality. Sometimes one has to drop the other because the other person really *is* messed up. Maybe he/she mistreats you, uses you, has an immoral life, etc. Then it is time to confront your partner on the particular issue. Breakees need to know why they are being rejected so they can learn from their mistakes. But do not impart negative information unless it is done in a gentle and humble spirit. Matthew 18:15-17 and Ephesians 4:15, 25-27 state the Christian principles in confronting those who have hurt you. 1) Keep the problem between yourselves—don't gossip and broadcast it; 2) Do not harbor grudges; confront the other person before Satan has an opportunity to weave sin into your anger; 3) Speak gently when confronting; 4) Do not consult others until the other person clearly continues to hurt himself and others; 5) Give your "breakee" time to answer. Talk it over. If you are going to get angry, take turns with each other. Don't get mad at the same time.

Advice to Both. After the break, clear your minds of each other. See each other only when necessary, and even then, keep conversation light and minimal. Do not be too friendly again too soon. The breakee may misconstrue that the two of you want to get back together.

Advice to Breakees

If your former lover is dropping you in such a way as to make you feel guilty or stupid, show him/her this chapter. If he refuses to read it, don't let your "ex's" immaturity be the cause of your emotional discomfort.

Prepare Yourself; Watch for the Signs. You may be able to see the breakup brewing: the blank stare, the "won't look into your eyes," an increase in the length and frequency of your fights, an undue amount of secrecy, flabby kisses (if they weren't that way before). Either ask your partner what is going on, or at least get your head prepared for an end to the relationship.

Let It Out. When you get dumped, do not be ashamed to be sad. Life as you have known it will be thrown out of balance. The sooner you release the grief you feel, the sooner you will feel stable again. Do not hold

back the tears, even if they come in the presence of your "ex." That goes for boys *and* girls. Crying is a natural way to relieve stress. If stress is not expressed one way, it will come out in others—sickness, bad dreams, the "grouchies." Talk it out with a trusted friend, too.

Mental Discipline. Bear in mind that your partner is not having any more fun telling you it is all over than you are in hearing it. Anger, resentment, and hostility do not have to be your immediate reactions. Be understanding. Listen carefully to what the breaker says. His explanation may be useful for your self-improvement. And above all, remember that just because one person in the world does not want you in a close, permanent relationship does not mean that nobody else does, or that you have no worth as a person.

Getting Rebalanced

The dirty work has been done. One of you has told the other, and both of you know that the relationship is all over. You may experience a real upset. Some people drop out of school or even kill themselves because they were dumped. Or you may meet the experience with just a twinge of loneliness, regret, indifference, or even relief. There are plenty of extremes and in-betweens in reactions to breakups. No matter what you feel, read on.

Rebalancing Breakers. Once you have made your decision to split up, **stick with it.** Maybe you do not hurt from the breakup, but your "ex" probably does, no matter how he/she may act in front of you. That means that any social contact you have with your old lover must be accompanied by utmost sensitivity and care.

Examine Yourself. You might not have had a breakup if you could have read personalities better.

Are you a poor judge of character? Or do you not know yourself? It may be either, both, or neither. And what that says is that you should take some time to **sort out why things went wrong.** Do not immediately seek another relationship.

Rebalancing Breakees. First of all, the above paragraph applies to you, too. **Get to know yourself** and be your own friend. Get some books on the subject of self-esteem and self-companionship. Learn to enjoy things on your own. Engage in recreation in group activities, particularly with members of your own sex. Renew the friendships you have. Go out and buy yourself something nice (but don't go into debt for it).

Secondly, if your recovery takes several months, **do not panic.** The pain you feel afterward is usually in direct proportion to the intensity of the relationship you have lost. Don't try to rush yourself. Just be sure that you are progressing in your independence.

Know when to quit. "Forgetting what is behind and straining toward what is ahead, I press on toward the goal to win the prize for which God has called me heavenward in Christ Jesus" (Philippians 3:13, 14, NIV). It is good to sort yourself out mentally; talk over the event with a trusted friend. But once you have faced the particulars and understand what happened and why, put the rejection experience out of your mind. There is a point at which "getting things off your chest" turns into basking in misery and bitterness. Know when to forget.

Get out among people. Do not sit and brood. Socializing will also help you to get the focus off yourself. Put some effort into helping others. Usually, you do not have to try very hard before meeting someone with a problem big enough for you to forget your own. I never met so many recently divorced people as the time I was bummed out from a broken engagement. Then I realized I was the lucky one.

Abide in the Word of God. The Bible has many comforting passages. Most of a breakee's problems and grief hinge on self-centeredness. God's Word has a way of turning you "inside out"; it helps you to quit looking at your own problems and instead focus on His magnificence and the needs of other fellow Christians and human beings.

Pray. Be honest. Bare your soul in prayer. You might as well. Tell God where you hurt. Seek His healing power. Ask Him to help you to understand why it happened. And as soon as you can honestly say so, thank Him for the breakup, both for what you have already gained from the experience, and also for the benefits yet to come. "And we know that in *all things* God works for the good of those who love him, who have been called according to his purpose" (Romans 8:28, NIV). That is a promise from God. Claim it!

#5
Questions to Consider

Questions 1—3, 6, 7 are designed to help reach a clearer perspective on the purposes or functions of breaking up. Questions 4 & 5 focus on the personal dynamics involved in a breakup and should help to appreciate one another's emotions and thought processes.

1. Do you think this book encourages breaking up too much? Why or why not?

2. Can you think of times when you broke up and you shouldn't have?

3. Can you think of times when you did not break up and you should have?

4. What hurts you most in a breakup?

5. Have you ever dropped anyone? How did you feel? How did the other person feel?

6. At what point in their relationship should a Christian break up with a non-Christian?

7. Are there times when you should break up even when you love each other? If you agree, what are some of these times?

Mini-Dramas

Select some examples of "breaker mistakes" and "breakee mistakes." Have couples from the group enact examples of them. Then have them repeat the skits with both members handling the situation maturely.